THE
ENCHANTED FOREST
COLORING BOOK

THE
ENCHANTED FOREST
COLORING BOOK

MARIA BRZOZOWSKA

SIRIUS

SIRIUS

This edition published in 2024 by Sirius Publishing, a division of
Arcturus Publishing Limited,
26/27 Bickels Yard, 151–153 Bermondsey Street,
London SE1 3HA

ISBN: 978-1-3988-3654-9
CH011809NT

Printed in China

INTRODUCTION

A wonderful collection of animals and magical creatures has made its home in the gloom of the enchanted forest and artist Maria Brzozowska has conjured a host of special scenes for you to color. To make your colors pop, each artwork has a dark background. You'll discover a social group of frogs gathered around a pond and busy beavers constructing their dams. You'll meet all kinds of birds, including predatory goshawks, woodpeckers, and songbirds such as robins, bullfinches, and siskins. And alongside the natural world are fantasy characters including flower fairies and forest elves. On the edge of the forest, a hare stares at the moon—a relationship as old as time. To make the most of these artworks, select pencils, pens, or markers in colors that will stand out against the background. Find a quiet spot (in a forest perhaps) and while away a couple of hours coloring your own enchanted world.

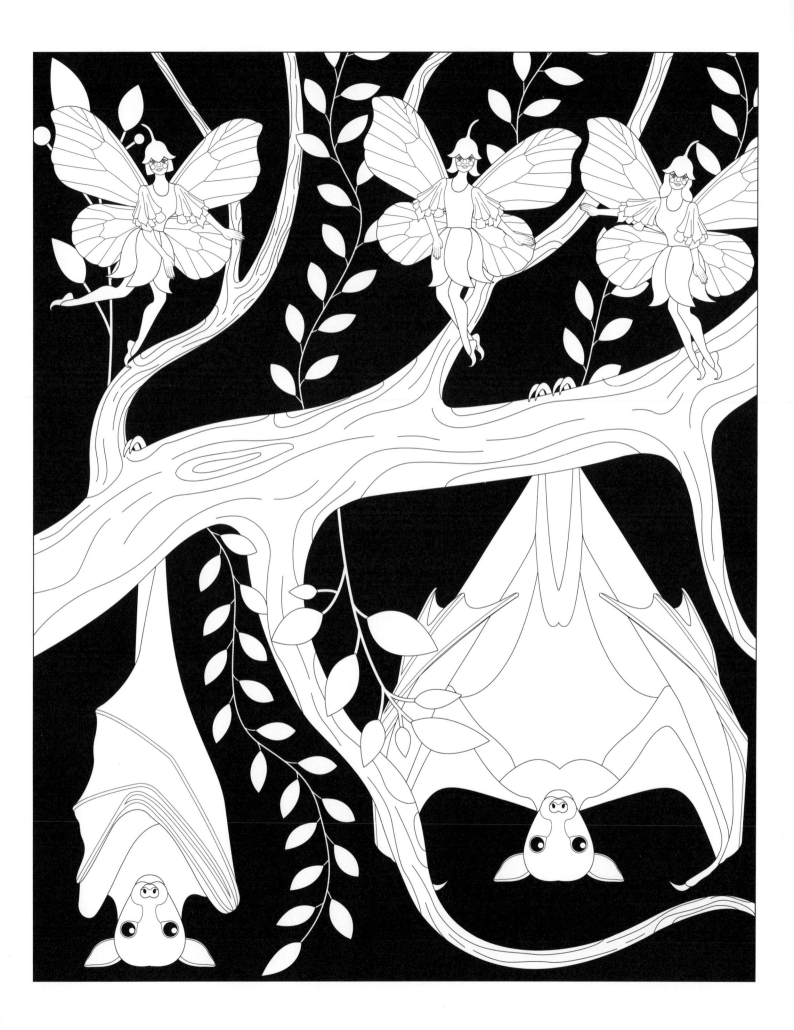

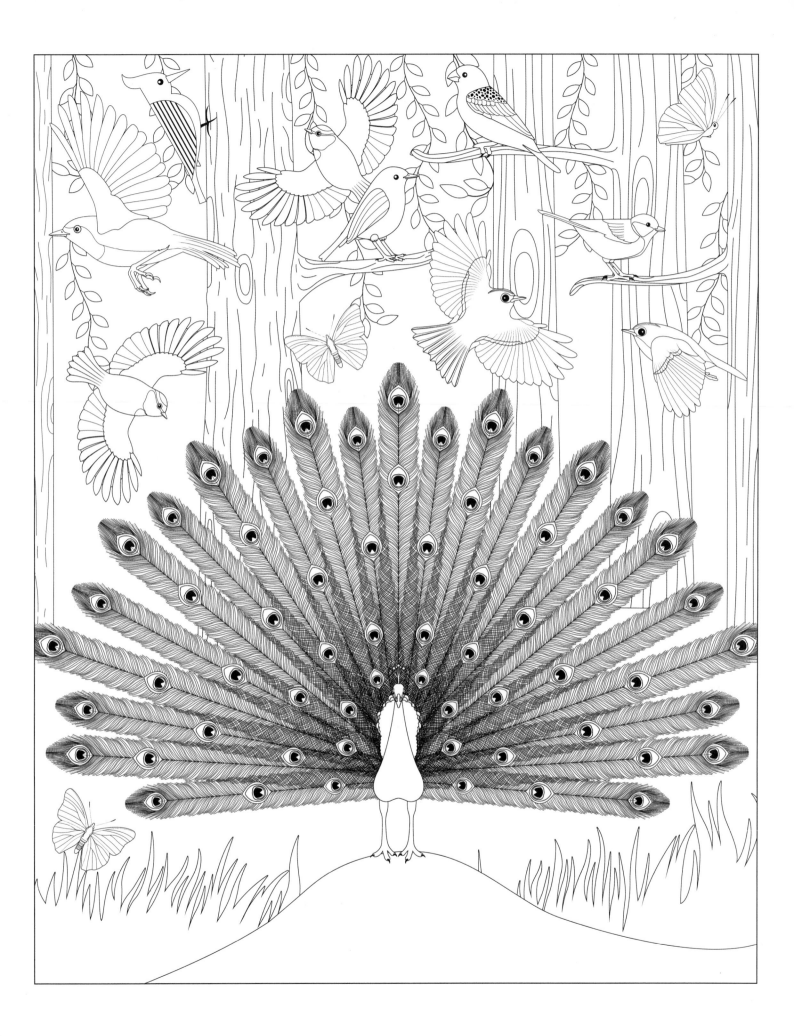